Mr Goril

Florence R McKay

MAPLE
PUBLISHERS

Mr Gorilla

Author: Florence R McKay

Illustrations by Noel D Mulvaney

Copyright © Florence R McKay (2022)

The right of Florence R McKay to be identified as author of this work has been asserted by the author in accordance with section 77 and 78 of the Copyright, Designs and Patents Act 1988.

First Published in 2022

ISBN 978-1-915164-63-6 (Paperback)

Published by:
    Maple Publishers
    1 Brunel Way,
    Slough,
    SL1 1FQ, UK
    www.maplepublishers.com

Book Layout by:
    White Magic Studios
    www.whitemagicstudios.co.uk

A CIP catalogue record for this title is available from the British Library.

All rights reserved. No part of this book may be reproduced or translated by any form or by any means, electronic or mechanical, including photocopying, recording or by any information storage and retrieval system without written permission from the author.

The views expressed in this work are solely those of the author and do not necessarily reflect the views of the publisher, and the publisher hereby disclaims any responsibility for them.

For the bot

Florence R McKay

My wardrobe is full of some crazy things, like socks so stinky that they have cheese trees growing on them, and a t-shirt so big that I have to ask a gorilla to sit in my wardrobe and wear it for me.

Mr Gorilla

Florence R McKay

A dress so bright and colourful you could get a tan, a pair of shorts so short that when I wear them you can see my bum, some mouldy vegetables I didn't want to eat last month and a pillow at the bottom of it all that gathers all the funny smells and dirt from the wardrobe.

Mr Gorilla

Which is why I was surprised that this morning I picked some completely ordinary clothes from the wardrobe. I popped on the clothes and they smelt and felt clean...ewwww I hate clean clothes!!!

Mr Gorilla

Florence R McKay

This morning mum made waffles
for breakfast, but when
I reached out to grab one...
I took a pear from the fruit
bowl instead.

Mr Gorilla

Florence R McKay

When I sat down to watch telly, I picked up my homework and started doing that. In my living room we have a very dusty shelf and as I walked past, a duster appeared in my hand and I started dusting. Not just the shelf, but every nook and cranny in the house, even the bathroom!

Mr Gorilla

Florence R McKay

When I went swimming with my friend everything went back to normal, I didn't dust anything, do any homework or anything in between. As I got changed back into my strange clean clothes they sparked and went on fire and we had to chuck the clothes into the swimming pool!

Mr Gorilla

Florence R McKay

When I finally got back home after getting clothes from the lost and found, I explained everything that happened to me that morning to the wise gorilla sitting in my wardrobe.

Mr Gorilla

The gorilla slowly replied, "it was your mums 'get things done t-shirt' that you picked out of the wardrobe this morning. When you got it wet, it set on fire because of the mini-machine inside it that made you do things around the house that you wouldn't usually do, like dusting".

Mr Gorilla

Florence R McKay

When mum put me to bed she thanked me for helping around the house, so now I do all the dusting, cleaning and eating healthy out of choice.

Mr Gorilla

Florence R McKay

P.S. if you were, or are, thinking about poor gorilla living in the wardrobe, Mr Gorilla sleeps on my bed.

CPSIA information can be obtained
at www.ICGtesting.com
Printed in the USA
LVHW071053050422
715335LV00007B/42